Multiply

Multiply

/////////////////////////////

A Gospel-Shaped Model for
Accomplishing God's Mission

ISAIAH PAULEY

FOREWORD BY SETH N. POLK

Sycamore
STORIES

Multiply: A Gospel-Shaped Model for Accomplishing God's Mission

Published by Sycamore Stories
Charleston, WV
sycamorestories.org

All Scripture quotations are taken from the Christian Standard Bible®, Copyright © 2020 by Holman Bible Publishers. Used by permission. Christian Standard Bible® and CSB® are federally registered trademarks of Holman Bible Publishers.

Cover image: Marlee Hope Photography
Author image: Jordon Pauley
Copy editing: Jonathan Wright
Interior design: Jonathan Lewis

Print information available on the last page.

Library of Congress Control Number: 2023920238

To my parents, James and Brooke Pauley.
Thank you for introducing me to Jesus.
To my grandmother, Mindy Kearns.
Thank you for helping me become a better writer.

Contents

//////////////////////////////

Foreword

///////////////////////////////////

I n *Multiply* Isaiah Pauley presents a model for discipleship in The Mission, The Model, and The Move. The Mission outlines God's plan for disciples to follow the Great Commission (Acts 1:8). The Model highlights the centrality of the gospel and how faith, and the grace of God are central in a relationship with Him (Matthew 22:34–40). Finally, The Move encourages action and moving forward in living out your calling from God (1 Corinthians 7:17–24). This is not a "try harder, do better" form of the Christian faith. Rather, the focus is on loving God and living for Him in total dependence on His power in our lives.

The essence of Christianity is life with God. The greatest need anyone has is to be in a right relationship with the Creator. God is holy, and we are sinful. Our sin separates us from God, resulting in spiritual death and eventually eternal separation. God sent His Son, Jesus, from heaven to earth to seek and save the lost (Luke 19:10). When we repent and believe in His death, burial, and resurrection, we enter into an eternal relationship with Him. Life with God is to be lived out as a disciple of Jesus.

A renewed emphasis on discipleship for followers of

Jesus has been seen in recent years. Life with God as a disciple of Jesus is clearly contrasted with what has been referred to as consumer Christianity. The terminology has been used by various writers in recent years.

Robby Gallaty identifies the difference between consumers and contributors and highlights the importance of discipleship:

1. Consumers are spectators. Contributors are participants.
2. Consumers see themselves as cisterns to store truth. Contributors see themselves as channels to bestow blessings.
3. Consumers criticize everything that doesn't line up with their preferences. Contributors appreciate what God is doing in the church.
4. Consumers come to "sit and get." Contributors look to go and serve.
5. Consumers take in only for themselves. Contributors pour out to others.

Gallaty concludes, "We must ensure that we understand the critical nature of the work of the gospel in the life of believers after salvation. When we understand that the gospel is not only for the lost, we will be able to lead people to Jesus and teach them to be like him."[1]

A focus on making disciples is more important than ever. The decline of Christianity in the West has been

---

[1] Robby Gallaty, "5 Differences between Ministry Consumers and Contributors," Lifeway Research (website), January 14, 2020, https://research.lifeway.com/2020/01/14/5-differences-between-ministry-consumers-and-contributors/.

evident in recent years. According to the Pew Research Center, "Since the 1990s, large numbers of Americans have left Christianity to join the growing ranks of U.S. adults who describe their religious identity as atheist, agnostic or 'nothing in particular.'"[2]

Pew Research Center projects that Christianity could potentially make up less than half of the U.S. population in just a few decades. Further, the Great Commission remains an unfinished task. There are 17,446 people groups in the world with 7,391 of those yet unreached.[3] The world needs Jesus, and His disciples have the privilege of making Him known!

Multiply is a Jesus-focused, grace-centered contribution to what it means to be a disciple. It is designed for implementation in student ministry, and the principles apply to all believers. The model may be applied in a variety of contexts to equip and encourage followers of Jesus. To reach a goal, we need to understand what the goal and preferred future are. The goal of discipleship is to become more like Jesus. "For those he foreknew he also predestined to be conformed to the image of his Son, so that he would be the firstborn among many brothers and sisters" (Romans 8:29). My prayer is that God will use the principles contained in this book to encourage reaching people for Jesus and growing disciples to be more like Him!

—Seth N. Polk, PhD

---

[2] "Modeling the Future of Religion in America," Pew Research Center (website), September 13, 2022, https://www.pewresearch.org/religion/2022/09/13/modeling-the-future-of-religion-in-america/.

[3] "Bringing Definition to the Unfinished Task," Joshua Project (website), accessed September 2, 2023, https://joshuaproject.net/.

Introduction

///////////////////////////

T he Multiply Model is a discipleship pathway. And it's not the only one out there. There are a whole bunch of them. You might be wondering why I'm introducing another one.

I became the student pastor of Cross Lanes Baptist Church (West Virginia) in June 2022, and I wanted to communicate a fresh and gospel-shaped strategy for discipling students. I sent a draft of the Multiply Model to my pastor, Seth Polk, in August 2022. His insights strengthened the model, and I introduced it to the students with a midweek series.

Later that year I tossed around the idea of putting the model into a short book to use as a small-group study for new students. I also wanted to have copies available for parents and anyone else in the church who wanted to know what we're about as a student ministry. So that's the primary reason you're holding this book in your hands. But it's not the only reason. You see, the Multiply Model isn't limited to student ministry.

No matter how young or old you are, God invites you to join Him on mission. And the Multiply Model can be applied in whatever context you find yourself. My prayer is that God would use this book to encourage individual Christians and churches alike. I've included questions and a prayer focus at the end of each chapter for personal or group reflection.

Whether you're reading this individually or with a small group, may God use it to give you clarity about His mission and how it is accomplished.

Truth be told, the Multiply Model is simple. It's just a fresh way of communicating what the church has been practicing for centuries. But a culture of gospel-shaped discipleship is lacking today. It's easier than ever to lose sight of what God is doing and the way in which He is doing it.

If your Christian life feels aimless, this book is for you. If your relationship with God seems stale, this book is for you. If you're a ministry leader needing some direction on discipleship, this book is for you.

God will show you how to apply this model in your context. For some it means a renewed focus on gospel teaching. For others it means a fresh approach to gospel community. Some may even come to realize that evangelism and discipleship play hardly any role at all in their understanding of God's mission.

So whatever the methods look like in your context, the model is meant to give you a framework for going about God's mission. Everything we do as followers of Christ should be intentional. We're not just doing stuff to say we're doing stuff.

For example, The Hill Students of Cross Lanes Baptist Church have several fun trips throughout the year. But those adventures are a method based on the second part of the Multiply Model called "Share Your Life." And the entire model is based on accomplishing God's mission as found in Acts 1:8. We communicate that mission in our context like this: "Making disciples from the hill to the valley and around the world."

The Multiply Model helps us stay focused on accomplishing God's plan for His glory. It reminds us that student ministry is more than games and activities. It reminds us to teach the entirety of God's Word. It reminds us to mobilize students for ministry and mission.

I've divided the book into three parts. The first part is meant to clarify God's mission. The second part is meant to provide a detailed explanation of the Multiply Model. And the third part is meant to help you make the move toward living it out.

I pray the lives, ministries, and churches influenced by this book engage in gospel-shaped discipleship for the glory of God. Now is the time to *multiply*!

The
Mission

1

God's Plan for You

///////////////////////////

Acts 1:8

We often view God's plan like a mystery to be solved rather than a mission to be accomplished.

Some people are obsessed with details. I'm one of those people. If something is off-centered, I notice it. If there's paint on the trim, I find it. Even when a professional contractor works on my house, I spot his errors almost immediately. By now some of you hope I never come to your house. But if it's any comfort to you, I never mention the things I see. I just obsess over them in my mind and totally miss the beauty of what's in front of me.

That's what happened the other day when my seminary degree came in the mail. The paper was slightly bent. That's the first thing I noticed. But it wouldn't be the last. I took it straight to my office and placed it in a frame. Only, I didn't line it up very well against the matting. And the degree slanted downward. My wife, Jordon, said it looked just fine. But I couldn't get it out of my head.

I ran a couple of miles, took a shower, and ate some dinner. I thought maybe that would help me forget about it. But it didn't. After putting my oldest boy, Dayton, to bed, I returned to the office at 8:30 p.m. with a tape measure in hand to straighten it out.

The next day I returned to the office and thought, *You know, that looks pretty good! It took me five years to get that!* I was so obsessed with the details that I missed the main point of it all.

As trivial as that story is, it's similar to the way we often think about God's plan. Sometimes we're so obsessed with the details that we totally miss the main point. We're busy playing our own little game of "This or That." This college or that college? This job or that job? This house or that house? This date or that date?

Dayton loves watching the television show *Mickey Mouse Clubhouse.* That means I hear it a lot. And the voices reside in my subconscious. As I write, I hear Donald Duck saying, "Hey—what's the big idea?" That's his catchphrase. It's not a bad question really. Trying so hard to decipher the details may cause us to miss the big idea.

You see, there is clarity in God's Word when it comes to God's plan for you. He cares about the details of your life. He really does. You should pray about them. You should seek counsel on them. But don't miss the main point of it all. God's plan for you is less about a mystery and more about a mission. As you follow His direction, He clarifies the details in His perfect time.

Jesus focuses His message and ministry on accomplishing the Father's plan. In Luke 19:10 He says, "The Son of Man has come to seek and to save the lost." Then, the book of Acts begins with a clear mandate for the mission of Jesus to move forward.

The church is given the job of continuing the mission of God in the world by making disciples who in turn make disciples. It's to *multiply*! But the world tries to distract us from this mission. Culture pulls us in and takes us away from the big idea. And it's hard to make progress when we're distracted.

We're pulled in by the latest stuff. We're distracted by what others think about us. We're taken off course when we look for happiness in the things of this world rather than Jesus. Before long, those distractions become the aim of our lives. They become the goalposts we run after, and they're always changing. So we're basically running aimlessly. And when this happens, we're going in the wrong direction. We're running away from God's plan.

God's plan for you is not an additional mission to add to your life. Rather, His plan must be *the* mission of your life. It must be your aim. And everything else falls into place.

Maybe you're struggling to surrender to God's plan for you. I know it's easier to cling to your own plan, to your own understanding of what you think will make you happy. But I hope this book helps you see that your greatest joy is found in submitting to the plan of God.

In Acts 1:8 Jesus tells His disciples, "You will receive power when the Holy Spirit has come on you, and you will be my witnesses in Jerusalem, in all Judea and Samaria, and to the ends of the earth."

Jesus had promised His disciples that upon His resurrection and ascension, the Holy Spirit would come to empower and guide them (Luke 24:49). Now Jesus is about to ascend to the Father in Acts 1:8. And He has much to say concerning God's plan for you.

God's plan for you is to rely on the Holy Spirit.

The only way to accomplish God's plan is by God's power. Otherwise, it's like trying to sail without wind or drive a car without gas.

If I stay awake all night, I'm not going to get out of bed in the morning. If I don't eat all day, I'm going to be "hangry" in the evening. Food and sleep are key to physical strength.

You and I need the Spirit of God to accomplish the mission of God. We might as well throw in the towel if we think we're going to pursue God's plan without His power.

Throughout the Book of Acts the disciples continue the mission of God. He uses them in mighty ways. But they don't rely on their own strength. God works through them because they rely on Him rather than themselves. In fact, the Bible identifies Peter and John in Acts 4:13 as uneducated, common men. *They* aren't great—but they have great *power*.

If you're a follower of Christ, you have the Spirit of God at work within you. One of the ways the Spirit works in your life is by empowering you to live on mission.

You may hear about God's plan for you and begin wondering if you have what it takes, if God can really use you to share the gospel with others. Remember: He sends you by going with you. You can rely on the Spirit to strengthen you for the work before you.

God's plan for you is to be a witness for Christ.

The task of a witness is to share what he or she has experienced. The earliest disciples of Jesus witnessed Him in the flesh. They saw Him with their own eyes, heard Him with their own ears, touched Him with their own hands. You and I haven't experienced Jesus like that. But to know Jesus is to have an experience worth sharing with others. You have something to witness about. You have a story to tell.

The disciples we read about in the Bible witnessed for Christ. They shared their faith. It often proved to be hard as they experienced great difficulty in sharing the gospel. Many of them even faced death for witnessing about Jesus. But they understood that regardless of the struggles and uncomfortable situations, God had called them to spread His message and make disciples.

That's the same mission you and I have today. And there's a purpose for it. God is glorified when the gospel is shared and people turn away from sin and believe in Christ.

Many people don't believe in Jesus, of course. God sends us to share Jesus with them in the power of the Spirit, to be witnesses for Him.

God's plan for you is to begin witnessing where you are.

In Acts 1:8 Jesus tells His followers to witness for Him in Jerusalem, Judea, Samaria, and to the ends of the earth. It's helpful to know that they're just outside of Jerusalem when Jesus gives this command. So Jesus is telling them to start where they are. That first step is instrumental in the spread of the gospel elsewhere.

This plan isn't only for the early disciples of Jesus. It's the mission He has for me and you. And it's still being accomplished today as the gospel is taken all over the world. You can start sharing Jesus right where you are.

You may read about God's plan and wonder where to start. It's a big plan. A plan including people from every language and nation. A plan with no cultural barriers.

I've taught the contents of this chapter to students in West Virginia, but I've also shared it with students and young adults in Lima, Peru. God's plan is for people everywhere. It reaches the entire world.

Even still, there's no need to be fearful or anxious. You don't need to be overwhelmed. You can begin witnessing where you are. Think about the opportunities you have each day to witness for Jesus. There's your home, your work, your school, your neighborhood.

God may give you the opportunity to witness in a different country one day. And I hope He does! But you must start where you are, asking Him to open your eyes to the work in front of you.

Conclusion

I hope by now you're starting to see just how clear God's plan is for you. And I know you have questions. I have questions too. But God answers our questions as we walk in what has been clearly given to us in His Word.

God's plan for you is to rely on the Holy Spirit, be a witness for Christ, and begin witnessing where you are.

His plans never fail (Acts 5:38–39). You can be sure of that. Over 2,000 years ago Jesus ascended to the Father. But His gospel is still advancing. Lives are still being changed. The church is still going strong. God's plan is moving forward—and there's a place for you in it.

You and I must lay down our own plans and submit to His. There's no time to waste. Our Master, Jesus Christ, is coming again. But there are plenty of other masters competing for our allegiance. That's what I want to focus on next.

Questions

1. What are some details you would like to know concerning God's plan for you? How do those details fit in the mission of God?
2. Do you live with an awareness of the Spirit's presence at work in your life? What difference does it make in pursuing God's plan for you?
3. What kind of role do you expect evangelism and discipleship to have in your future?
4. Think about where you are in this season of life. Can you identify some people around you who need Jesus? What are some steps you can take today to share Him with those people?
5. Does God's plan for you interfere with your own plan for yourself?

Prayer Focus

Thank God for making His plan for you clear. Ask Him for the faith to believe that His plans are better than yours.

2

Mission and Master

////////////////////////////////

Matthew 6:24

Idols take the best from us and bring out the worst in us. They require our best energy and efforts. They cause our greatest fears and frustrations.

Take the golden calf, for example. The Israelites grew impatient with Yahweh and decided to make themselves a god. It took the best of their gold and craftsmanship, the best of their singing and shouting—until Moses burned the idol to the ground and scattered the ashes in their drinking water. Then he stood at the gate and said, "Whoever is for the Lord, come to me" (Exodus 32:26). The Levites came and killed the idolatrous. Three thousand died.

Most of our idols today are morally neutral and subtle in nature. But they're just as dangerous. They're just as deadly.

In His Sermon on the Mount (Matthew 5–7), Jesus communicated the nature of His kingdom. It's unlike this world. He said, "No one can serve two masters, since either he will hate one and love the other, or he will be devoted to one and despise the other. You cannot serve both God and money" (Matthew 6:24). Life is a battlefield of competing passions and pursuits. Thankfully, we're given a clear mission in Acts 1:8. This must be what calibrates the life of a Christian. When our passions and pursuits run contrary to this mission, we need a recalibration.

We must keep _____ (fill in the blank) subjected to the mission rather than allowing it to become the master.

When it becomes the master, God gets pushed aside. Our devotion to Him turns into disgust, and we live fearful, frustrated, and unsatisfied lives. Yet this is the kind of life we often promote, even if unintentionally, a life of unfit masters taking us away from the mission of God. What are some of these unfit masters? Usually they're not as obvious as a golden calf—but they're just as capable of destroying our devotion to God and His mission.

In *The Cost of Discipleship* Dietrich Bonhoeffer writes, "Our hearts have room only for one all-embracing devotion, and we can only cleave to one Lord. Every competitor to that devotion must be hated."[1]

Truth be told, most of our unfit masters aren't wrong in and of themselves. That's what makes them so easy to follow. Five unfit masters come to mind. Let's start with the one Jesus mentions in Matthew 6:24.

Money

We must keep money subjected to the mission rather than

---

[1] Dietrich Bonhoeffer, *The Cost of Discipleship* (New York: Touchstone, 1959), 176.

allowing it to become the master. Several other masters come from the worship of money.

In his first letter to Timothy, Paul writes, "The love of money is a root of all kinds of evil, and by craving it, some have wandered away from the faith and pierced themselves with many griefs" (1 Timothy 6:10).

The rich young man in Matthew 19 walked away from Jesus because money was his master. His assets were great. In Luke 12 Jesus shared a parable about a rich man who sought to accumulate as much as possible.

Ecclesiastes 5:10 says, "The one who loves silver is never satisfied with silver, and whoever loves wealth is never satisfied with income."

Money is a brutal master. But when it's subjected to the mission it's a powerful tool. Everything belongs to God. We're stewards. If our aim in life is to be rich, we're bound for disappointment. But if we keep money subjected to the mission, we can steward it well for His glory. And that's true whether it's a lot of money or hardly any at all.

Education

Some view education as the way to success, the means of truth, capable of leading one to a satisfying life. But only Jesus can do that. We must keep education subjected to the mission rather than allowing it to become the master.

The Bible speaks highly of education, but there's a purpose for it. Education serves calling and assignment in accomplishing God's mission. Some callings and assignments require more education than others. A person without a high school diploma can be just as successful for Christ as a doctor. Education is not the passport to a satisfying life, even though some would have us believe it is.

Ecclesiastes 12:12 says, "Beyond these, my son, be warned: there is no end to the making of many books, and much study wearies the body."

If our aim in life is education, we're sure to be disappointed. But if we keep education subjected to the mission, it becomes an immensely helpful tool in fulfilling our callings and assignments. That's true whether it's a lot of education or hardly any at all. And when it comes to deciding on a college or another type of post-secondary education, the mission of God should be our primary concern, particularly as it relates to our engagement in a local church.

Work

God has always intended for us to work. Genesis 2:15 says, "The Lord God took the man and placed him in the garden of Eden to work it and watch over it."

He calls us to work hard. Colossians 3:23 says, "Whatever you do, do it from the heart, as something done for the Lord and not for people."

Typically, work is intricately connected to money and education. To idolize one is to easily idolize another. We must keep work subjected to the mission rather than allowing it to become the master.

The predominant view in culture is thinking too little of work. But there are certainly those who think too highly of it, counting on a job to satisfy, centering their lives around what they do rather than what God has done for them.

Work is yet another brutal master. It demands time that should be spent elsewhere. Of course, everyone has busy seasons. A job is sure to require some inconvenient hours. And yes—a job well done brings a feeling of satisfaction. But centering our lives on work equates to not centering our lives on Christ.

Family

Family is a gift from God. Marriage is a beautiful picture of the gospel (Ephesians 5:22–33). Parents are to raise their children in the ways of God (Ephesians 6:4; Deuteronomy 6:7). Children are to honor their parents (Ephesians 6:1–3; Exodus 20:12). And parents eventually let their children go (Genesis 2:24).

An interesting story is found in Matthew 8. A disciple comes to Jesus and asks to bury his father before following Jesus. That's when Jesus says, "Follow me, and let the dead bury their own dead" (v. 22).

Some say the man wanted to bury his dead father immediately. Others say he was requesting to refrain from following Jesus until his father died.[2] Either way, we're reminded of just how serious the mission of God is. We must keep family subjected to the mission rather than allowing it to become the master.

Only God can give us the wisdom to understand how these verses fit together. For example, should a missionary serving in China return to the United States to care for parents or continue following Jesus where he or she is?

I'm not trying to oversimply this. It can be difficult to determine how the pieces fit together. But generally, when God calls you to serve Him, family ties shouldn't

---

[2] David Platt, *Exalting Jesus in Matthew*, Christ-Centered Exposition, eds. David Platt, Daniel L. Akin, and Tony Merida (Nashville: Holman, 2013), 112–113.

get in the way. Jesus is making it clear in Matthew 8 that following Him may result in an uncomfortable distance between child and parent. And I don't believe this is only true for pastors and missionaries.

The primary factor in determining where you live and work must be the mission of God. It's possible to short-circuit what God wants to do in your life because of an attachment to parents or extended family.

For the sake of clarity, I love my parents a lot. I live an hour away from them and still see them quite often. When God called me and Jordon to Cross Lanes, it was difficult for them. But even family must be subjected to the mission of God.

In Matthew 10:37 Jesus said, "The one who loves a father or mother more than me is not worthy of me; the one who loves a son or daughter more than me is not worthy of me." When family is the master, we're unwilling to follow Jesus wherever He calls us. For some that's another city, another state. For others it's another country. For most it's simply committing to a local church and living missionally regardless of the example set in previous generations.

It's also worth noting that when we come to know God by grace through faith in Christ, we become members of God's family. And this family is eternal. It's based on the gospel, not on flesh and blood. Jesus emphasizes the priority of this eternal, gospel-based family in Matthew 12:50 when he says, "Whoever does the will of my Father in heaven is my brother and sister and mother."

The vision of Cross Lanes Baptist Church is "Growing God's Forever Family." It's not only a reminder to us of the eternal nature of God's family, but it's also a call for us to invite others to belong to this family by grace through faith in Christ that they too might abide and produce fruit in Him (John 15:5).

Recreation

It's a simple truth that some people are ruled by a master called recreation. Activities like sports, music, travel, hobbies, and others easily distract us from the mission of God.

One of the ways we know it's a problem is when it takes us away from church multiple times a year. But it's more than that. When recreation is the master of our lives, it has our greatest affections, time, energy, and resources. We must keep recreation subjected to the mission rather than allowing it to become the master.

In high school I played two sports and participated in multiple academic clubs. It's possible to be engaged in those things and still be committed to a local church.

Ecclesiastes 3:1 says, "There is an occasion for everything, and a time for every activity under heaven." There's a time for vacation. There's a time for hobbies. But to repeatedly miss worship and discipleship opportunities for some type of recreation is exactly what the master called "recreation" wants.

When recreation is the master of your life, God's mission gets pushed aside. You don't commit. You don't serve. And you don't grow in Christ the way you should.

Conclusion

This has been a difficult chapter to write. Money, education, work, family, and recreation are touchy subjects. These things matter to all of us. And that's why it's so easy to let them become the masters of our lives.

If you're going to embrace God's plan for you, you are required to pursue His mission above anything and anyone else. God must be the Master of your life. And Jesus says you can't serve two masters.

The mission is clear. The cost of following Jesus is great. But how is someone led to become a disciple who makes disciples? How does multiplication occur in the context of our daily lives? That's where the Multiply Model comes into play.

Questions

1. Idolatry comes from the heart. What does it say about the way you view God and His mission if you're unwilling to let go of something else to pursue Him more fully?

2. How have you seen money, education, work, family, and recreation subjected to God's mission and therefore helpful in accomplishing it?

3. To push God aside and replace Him with another master is to lose sight of His mission and what life is all about. What does it look like for you to grow in love and devotion to God each day?

4. Read Matthew 6:21 and 6:33. These verses come in the context of 6:24. What do you prize the most and seek the most?

5. Submitting your life to God and laying down your own plans is difficult. How does Matthew 16:24 relate to this?

Prayer Focus

Thank God for the eternal life He provides by grace through

faith in Christ. Ask Him to help you love Him and pursue Him more than anything or anyone else.

The Model

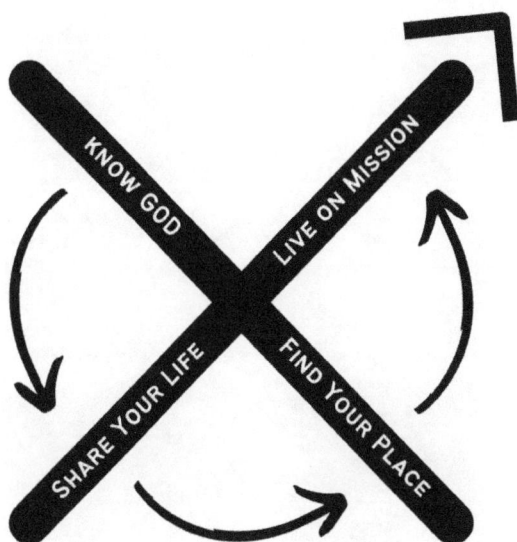

3

Know God

///////////////////////////////

Matthew 22:34-40

God is knowable because He makes Himself known.
There's His general revelation and His special revelation. His creation is an example of His general revelation (Romans 1:20). But His Word is the special revelation. This includes the written Word of God (2 Timothy 3:16–17) and the Word made flesh (John 1:14).

God has taken the initiative. There's a way for me and you to know Him—and it's only by grace through faith in His Son, Jesus Christ.

I was raised in a small West Virginia town by faithful parents who introduced me to Christ as a young child. My mom led me in a prayer of repentance and faith when I was five. I was baptized a couple of years later in believer's baptism.

There's nothing I've done to earn my salvation. It's all of grace. As I've abided in Christ and grown in relationship with God, it has become even clearer to me that life with God isn't about trying harder and doing better. It's about resting in the accomplishment of Christ and trusting in Him to fuel my own obedience.

When the Bible begins, Adam and Eve are in perfect relationship with God—until they sin. That's when their relationship with Him is severed, as Genesis 3 describes. But God makes a promise in Genesis 3:15 when He says the seed of the woman will crush the head of the serpent. This is considered the protoevangelium, the first mention of the gospel.

Throughout the Old Testament God works with this promise in mind. He promises to bless the nations through Abraham's offspring (Genesis 12:3). He promises to provide an eternal King through the lineage of David (2 Samuel 7:16). When the New Testament opens, it becomes clear that Jesus Christ is the one who comes through the seed of the woman. He is the one through whom the nations are blessed (Revelation 7:9–10). He is the eternal King (Revelation 20–22). And it's only by turning from sin and believing in the sufficiency of Jesus Christ's death, burial, and resurrection that we can be reconciled to God, taking part in the victory of the gospel.

So it's not something we can accomplish ourselves. It comes by grace alone through faith alone in Christ alone (Ephesians 2:8–10).

Charles Spurgeon writes, "Do not attempt to touch yourself up and make yourself something other than you really are, but come as you are, to Him who justifies the ungodly."[1]

---

[1] C. H. Spurgeon, *All of Grace: An Earnest Word with Those Who Are Seeking Salvation by the Lord Jesus Christ* (Chicago: Moody Publishers, 2010), 34.

My aim in this chapter is to help us understand what it means to know God.

The mission of God is clear—to make disciples who make disciples. It's to *multiply*. But knowing God is where it starts. That's why it's the first part of the Multiply Model. Whether you're an unbeliever yourself or sharing your faith with another, it begins with knowing God. And those who know Him must share Him with others.

To quote Spurgeon again, "Soul-winning is the chief business of the Christian minister; it should be the main pursuit of every true believer."[2]

Accomplishing the mission of God requires evangelism (Romans 10:14–15). The gospel must be explained correctly. An invitation must be given for people to know God through Christ. That's why it's so important for the Word to be taught in a gospel-shaped way. This is true for our churches, ministries, and personal evangelism. If we skip this step, we don't accomplish the mission of God.

So let's dig into Matthew 22:34–40 to see what it means to know God. First, it's important to understand what it doesn't mean.

To know Scripture does not necessarily mean to know God.

In verses 34–36 some Pharisees come together to test Jesus. Matthew is sure to inform us of how the Sadducees are silenced by Jesus. He does so in verses 23–33 when the Sadducees come to Jesus and ask Him a question about the resurrection, something the Sadducees do not believe

---

[2] C. H. Spurgeon, *The Soulwinner* (New Kensington, PA: Whitaker House, 1995), 7.

in. They question Jesus by offering a scenario that at first glance seems to be at odds with the resurrection of the dead. Jesus silences them by stating the reality of the resurrection despite the misunderstanding they have.

The Pharisees aren't fans of the Sadducees, so they likely enjoy how Jesus corrects them. But they too get together and decide to test Jesus. One of the Pharisees considered as an expert in the law asks, "Teacher, which command in the law is the greatest?" (v. 36).

By "law," the Pharisee is referring to Scripture. D. A. Carson sheds some light on this when he writes, "The 'law,' of course, is Scripture, especially the Pentateuch. But because Scripture was applied to every area of life—including all civil matters—by means of certain interpretative rules and a vast complex of tradition, such an expert was, by modern standards, both a learned theologian and a legal expert."[3] And this expert of Scripture is trying to trip Jesus up.

The gospels make it clear as to how the religious leaders knew a lot about God and His Word. But they did not know God Himself. For example, in John 5:38–40 Jesus says, "You don't have his word residing in you, because you don't believe the one he sent. You pore over the Scriptures because you think you have eternal life in them, and yet they testify about me. But you are not willing to come to me so that you may have life." We must beware of knowing a lot about God without really knowing Him at all. In his book *Knowing God*, J. I. Packer writes, "A

---

[3] D. A. Carson, *Matthew*, The Expositor's Bible Commentary, ed. Frank E. Gaebelein (Grand Rapids: Zondervan, 1984), 464.

little knowledge *of* God is worth more than a great deal of knowledge *about* him."[4]

Just because someone can quote a lot of Scripture doesn't mean he or she knows God. Just because someone can engage in deep theological discussion doesn't mean he or she knows God.

There's a difference between knowing God and knowing *about* God. The religious leaders knew Scripture well. But they did not know *God* because they rejected His Son. They failed to realize how the law and the prophets pointed to Christ.

So as we consider what it means to know God, it's important for us to recognize this flaw in the Pharisee who tried to test Jesus with a question and to recognize how his knowledge of Scripture did not indicate a knowledge of God Himself.

Scripture does have a central role in our understanding of God. But just because we know the Bible doesn't mean we know God. The goal, then, is not simply teaching God's Word. It's also to help others know God. And this extends beyond the mind to also impact the heart and soul as we begin to see in the response Jesus gave to the Pharisee.

To know God means to love God and others.

Jesus turned the Pharisee's attention to the *Shema*. That's a Hebrew word referring to the process of hearing, found in Deuteronomy 6. Verses 4 and 5 say, "Listen, Israel: The Lord our God, the Lord is one. Love the Lord your

---

[4] J. I. Packer, *Knowing God*, Anniversary ed. (Downers Grove, IL: InterVarsity Press, 1993), 26.

God with all your heart, with all your soul, and with all your strength."

Devout Jews pray the Shema even today. It remains a big part of their worship. I had an Old Testament professor who required us to open each class by reciting Deuteronomy 6:4–5 in Hebrew!

Jesus was taking a well-known and much-loved prayer from the Old Testament and telling the Pharisee that this was the Great Commandment—which, of course, was the answer to the Pharisee's question.

Then He gave him a second command by turning the Pharisee's attention to another Old Testament passage, Leviticus 19:18—"Do not take revenge or bear a grudge against members of your community, but love your neighbor as yourself; I am the Lord."

Love God. Love others. That's the idea. It speaks of relationship. And it's this relationship the religious leaders lacked. They knew Deuteronomy 6. They knew Leviticus 19. But they did not know God because they did not accept Jesus, who revealed God.

In 1 John 4:9–10 we read, "God's love was revealed among us in this way: God sent his one and only Son into the world so that we might live through him. Love consists in this: not that we loved God, but that he loved us and sent his Son to be the atoning sacrifice [propitiation] for our sins."

Knowing God without Jesus doesn't work. *Loving* God without Jesus doesn't work. Jesus has revealed God to us. He has shown us what love is.

The Pharisee, then, doesn't know God if he rejects Christ. And he doesn't love God with all his heart, soul, and mind if he rejects Christ. He may be an expert. He might have a big brain. But if he rejects the Messiah, his mind isn't in sync with the gospel. As long as he rejects the Messiah, his heart and soul are not affectionate about the mission of God. And this lack of relationship with God influences the lack of love he shows to others.

Knowing God means having a relationship with God, to love Him and in turn to love others. When this happens, the Great Commandment is followed. But this relationship is possible only through the person and work of Christ. Our obedience relies on Him.

To love God and others means to obey Scripture through Christ.

Jesus summed up His response to the Pharisee when He said in verse 40, "All the Law and the Prophets depend on these two commands."

As I said earlier, the Law and the Prophets essentially refer to Scripture. This is what the Pharisees regarded as Scripture. So in their understanding, Jesus was saying the Scripture depended on these two commands. But what did He mean by "depend on"? Another way of saying it is "hang on." The Scripture hangs on the commands to love God and love people.

Again, D. A. Carson is helpful when he writes, "These two commandments are the greatest because all Scripture hangs on them, i.e., nothing in Scripture can cohere or be truly obeyed unless these two are observed."[5]

Jesus said in John 14:15, "If you love me, you will keep

---

[5] D. A. Carson, *Matthew*, The Expositor's Bible Commentary, 464.

my commands." To know God is to love God. And to love God is to obey God.

But this knowledge, this love, and this obedience come through Christ. It's important to understand how Jesus Christ fulfills the Law and the Prophets. He is what Scripture points to. He is the one who loves His Father perfectly—and loves others perfectly. He is the perfect one who fully obeyed. And now, through Him—because He took care of our sins by shedding His blood on the cross—we can know God in love and obedience.

In Matthew 5:17 Jesus said, "Don't think that I came to abolish the Law or the Prophets. I did not come to abolish but to fulfill."

So Jesus fulfills the Law and Prophets. And it's the Law and the Prophets that hang on the commands to love God and love people.

If we're going to obey Scripture, it must come through Christ, who fulfilled the Law and the Prophets for us. It's only through Him that we can know God and love as He requires. And we love, as 1 John 4:19 says, because He first loved us.

The goal is not that we would simply know Scripture but that we obey it—in love for God and others. This is possible only through Christ. And we experience that relationship with God as we come to Jesus in faith and repentance.

Conclusion

Obedience to the Great Commandment in Matthew 22:34–40 results in obedience to the Great Commission of Matthew 28:18–20.

There's only one way to know God. There's only one way to truly love God and others. And it comes by grace through faith in Christ. To know God means to love God and others in obedience to Scripture through Christ.

Maybe you're reading this today and you've never turned from your sin. You've never placed your faith in Jesus. Don't put it off! It's a great day to be saved. Romans 10:9 promises, "If you confess with your mouth, 'Jesus is Lord,' and believe in your heart that God raised him from the dead, you will be saved."

For those of us who do know God, let's never get past the beauty of the gospel. Let's abide in Jesus. Let's see God's forever family grow.

In fact, those who know God are called to live for Him in relationship with others who know Him. And that's the next part of the Multiply Model.

Questions

1. What does it look like to rest in the finished work of Christ rather than viewing your life with God as a religious checklist?
2. Why is it easy for us to become more concerned with what we know *about* God than with knowing God Himself?
3. Does the way you treat others display the gospel or discard the gospel?
4. How does studying the Bible and hearing it taught play a role in knowing God?
5. Are you actively striving to help others know God by grace through faith? What are some different ways to evangelize?

Prayer Focus

Thank God for the relationship you have with Him. Ask
Him to draw you closer as you look to Jesus and become
more and more like Him.

4

Share Your Life

/////////////////////////////

Acts 2:42–47

I recently put some patio furniture together on my back porch—and I'm not very good at putting stuff together.

While struggling to assemble the furniture, I noticed my neighbor walking toward me with a little case of tools in his hand. He put them on my porch and said I could use them if I needed them. It felt unnatural to me. Not because it was wrong. It was nice of him to offer me his tools. But I didn't expect it. And I never would have thought of doing the same for someone else (partly because I don't have any tools).

We live in an increasingly individualistic culture. We don't like to share. I vaguely remember a time when each home had one TV set, one phone on the wall, one CD player, and one gigantic computer. It's a lot different now. I'm typing this on my own laptop with my own phone and earbuds beside me.

The individualism we're accustomed to influences how we view our spiritual lives and the relationships we have with fellow believers—so much so that if we're not careful, we miss the significance of sharing life with one another as brothers and sisters in Christ, becoming enamored by our own spiritual experiences.

But we're made in the image of a Triune God (Genesis 1:27), one God in three persons. I know it's hard to wrap our minds around. But there's fellowship in the Trinity. The overflow of that joyful fellowship is an opportunity for those who know God to share life with Him and His people. Discipleship doesn't happen in a vacuum.

In Acts 2:42–47 we find a beautiful picture of what it means to share your life with other believers.

To share your life means to hold on to the gospel.

The devotion of the early church is rooted in the message of the apostles and the implications of that message.

Verses 42 and 43 say, "They devoted themselves to the apostles' teaching, to the fellowship, to the breaking of bread, and to prayer. Everyone was filled with awe, and many wonders and signs were being performed through the apostles."

The teaching was that of Jesus Christ and Him crucified, buried, risen, and ascended. That's the sermon Peter preached at Pentecost, using the Old Testament to point to Christ, helping them see the connection. And the apostles were eyewitnesses to this reality.

In Acts 2 Paul is still Saul. But in 1 Corinthians 15:1–8 the apostle Paul gives us a clear picture of the gospel message preached to the early followers of Christ.

The Barna Group conducted a study in 2022 of how teens around the world relate to Jesus. They surveyed over 24,000 teens from twenty-six different countries.

Interestingly, they found that 52 percent of teens call themselves Christians. But only 50 percent of those who identify as such believe in the resurrection of Jesus. And only 44 percent believe in the incarnation of Jesus.

In an article reflecting on this research, Nick Hartman sums it up well: "Teenagers call themselves Christians but don't know the Gospel."[1] I can't even begin to describe just how much of a problem that is—because it's the gospel we *need!*

The early church was devoted to the gospel, not only in the teaching but also in the fellowship, breaking of bread, and prayer.

The word *fellowship* is a Greek word that literally means "sharing." These early followers of Jesus devoted themselves to gospel community. They did not try living out their faith by themselves. And the same must be true of us. We're not meant to live our lives removed from other believers.

The same Barna study states, "Three in five Bible-engaged teens have received help studying the Bible from a parent/guardian. These teens say a pastor, priest, or ministry, Bible study group/leader or Sunday school teacher also contributed to their understanding of the Bible."[2]

It's the beauty of discipleship. And that fellowship

---

[1] Nick Hartman, "A Reflection on Barna's Open Generation Report," Youth Pastor Theologian (website), October 26, 2022, https://www.youthpastortheologian.com/blog/a-reflection-on-barnas-open-generation-report.

[2] Ibid.

is rooted in the gospel. It's not that we're simply get-
ting together to *say* we're together. It's that our common
ground—our unity—is found in Christ.

It's believed that the reference here to the breaking of
bread is in some way referring to the Lord's Supper, a visual
reminder of the gospel. We take the Lord's Supper and
remember the body and blood of Christ (1 Corinthians
11:23–26). We remember the gospel we hold on to. And
we anticipate the return of our Lord and Savior.

The early disciples devoted themselves to prayer too.
It's communal. They prayed as one.

Dietrich Bonhoeffer wrote, "The physical presence of
other Christians is a source of incomparable joy and strength
to the believer. . . . The believer feels no shame, as though
he were still living too much in the flesh, when he yearns for
the physical presence of other Christians. . . . The prisoner,
the sick person, the Christian in exile sees in the compan-
ionship of a fellow Christian a physical sign of the gracious
presence of the Triune God."[3]

Gospel community is an amazing thing. Don't take it
for granted.

To share your life means to hold your possessions loosely.

The disciples in Acts 2 were not stingy with what they had.
They were generous, ready to share because they realized
the mission at hand.

Acts 2:44–45 explains, "Now all the believers were
together and held all things in common. They sold their

possessions and property and distributed the proceeds to all, as any had need."

When we share our lives, we live with open hands. Rather than holding our stuff tightly, we want to steward what we have for the glory of God and the advancement of His mission.

God gave us His one and only Son. He made a way for us to be included in this fellowship. Why? Because He loves us. He wants us to enjoy fellowship with Him and with our brothers and sisters in Christ.

Think about everything Christ sacrificed for us. Philippians 2:5–8 says, "Adopt the same attitude as that of Christ Jesus who, existing in the form of God, did not consider equality with God as something to be exploited. Instead he emptied himself by assuming the form of a servant, taking on the likeness of humanity. And when he had come as a man, he humbled himself by becoming obedient to the point of death—even to death on a cross."

Jesus never lost His divinity by coming to earth. Paul was emphasizing the humility of Jesus in these verses. He gave His life that we might have life with God. Similarly, 2 Corinthians 8:9 says, "For you know the grace of our Lord Jesus Christ: Though he was rich, for your sake he became poor, so that by his poverty you might become rich."

Are you living life with open hands or holding tightly to what you possess? The early church was a generous church, sharing life and possessions. You see, everything we think we own is actually God's. We're just stewards.

Are you allowing God to use what you have for His glory and the accomplishment of His mission?

Paul writes in 2 Corinthians 9:7, "Each person should

do as he has decided in his heart—not reluctantly or out of compulsion, since God loves a cheerful giver."

The early believers came together with a tight grip on the gospel and a loose grip on their possessions. And there was a purpose behind it. They were on mission, devoted to living out the gospel.

We see this not only in how they handled their possessions but also in how they handled their time.

To share your life means to hold your time loosely.

They surrendered their possessions, but they also gave their time. They made sharing life with brothers and sisters in Christ a top priority. We see this in their daily meeting together and sharing of meals.

Verses 46 and 47 say, "Every day they devoted themselves to meeting together in the temple, and broke bread from house to house. They ate their food with joyful and sincere hearts, praising God and enjoying the favor of all the people. Every day the Lord added to their number those who were being saved."

It was a community living with open hands, open homes, and prioritized schedules. Sharing life takes time. It takes proper stewardship of both possessions and time for the sake of advancing God's mission.

These early followers of Jesus were engaged in daily evangelism, and the Lord added to their number each day. How often do we find it hard to make time for evangelism and discipleship? We find it hard to spend time with God's people, let alone share the gospel with unbelievers. These moments are a sign that we're holding our time too tightly.

I love how Paul puts it in his letter to the church at Thessalonica: "We cared so much for you that we were pleased to share with you not only the gospel of God but also our own lives, because you had become dear to us" (1 Thessalonians 2:8).

The author of Hebrews also emphasizes the importance of coming together often when he writes, "Let us hold on to the confession of our hope without wavering, since he who promised is faithful. And let us consider one another in order to provoke love and good works, not neglecting to gather together, as some are in the habit of doing, but encouraging each other, and all the more as you see the day approaching" (10:23–25).

We spend time doing the things we find most important. Is it important to you that you're spending time with your brothers and sisters in Christ? Remember—they are fellow members of God's family. Those who know God are being shaped by the gospel. Sharing life with other believers is one of the ways God conforms us to the image of His Son.

Conclusion

We're created in the image of a Triune God who is Himself a beautiful fellowship of love. To know God by grace through faith in Christ is to have the joy of partaking in this eternal fellowship. Along with this comes a fellowship with others who know Him.

Gospel multiplication relates to the sharing of life. In Acts 2 the church grew because those who knew God came together as disciples who strived to make disciples. To share your life means to hold on to the gospel and hold your possessions and time loosely.

Sharing life with other believers is essential to your own discipleship and the calling you have to make disciples. As you share your life, it becomes evident that you have a part to play in the community of believers. You're not meant to simply sit on the sidelines in accomplishing God's mission. And that's the subject of what comes next in the Multiply Model.

Questions

1. What is your experience as it relates to sharing life with other believers? How have you seen it done well? How have you seen it done poorly?
2. Can you think of some reasons we're tempted not to share life with others?
3. Can you think of some practical opportunities you have to share life with other believers?
4. What does it look like for you to hold your possessions and time loosely? Why are we often prone to hold them tightly instead?
5. What are some things we base our community on each day? Do you think we ever try to replace the gospel with those things?

Prayer Focus

Thank God for the joy of sharing life with Him and His people. Ask Him to help you let go of what you need to let go of to share your life even more.

5

Find Your Place

1 Peter 4:10–11

Nobody likes to feel out of place. Usually it results in a quick departure. When Dayton was born, I got lost in the hospital and found myself in a restricted access zone. I still don't know how I got there. But I escaped as fast as I could. I had no scrubs. I had no badge. And I certainly lacked the appropriate medical knowledge to be there. I simply didn't belong.

Those who feel connected are more likely to stay. This is true in several areas of our lives. The athlete who never gets to play is more likely to quit. Those who never get the opportunity to contribute eventually begin to wonder if they even matter at all.

Believers who feel as if they don't belong to the church are more likely to quit coming. Notice how I say *believers*. The foundation of our belonging is the gospel of Jesus Christ. That's where our unity comes from.

I've heard it said that unbelievers coming to church should

feel as if they "belong before they believe." The idea behind this statement is a desire to show warm hospitality to those visiting. And, of course, we should make them feel welcomed and loved. But to say they belong before they believe is dangerous. Unbelievers will not feel as if they belong to the body of Christ unless they find their identity in Christ.

Believers have a part to play in how the mission of God is being accomplished. They have a place in the local church. There's work for them to do.

According to Lifeway Research, "Two-thirds (66 percent) of American young adults who attended a Protestant church regularly for at least a year as a teenager say they also dropped out for at least a year between the ages of 18 and 22."

There are various reasons for this. But one of them is a lack of connection to the believers in their congregation. In fact, Lifeway says 29 percent of those who stopped attending church as 18- to 22-year-olds mention a lack of connection to others in the church as a reason for dropping out.

Scott McConnell says, "As those teenagers reach their late teen years, even those with a history of regular church attendance are pulled away as they get increased independence, a driver's license, or a job."

Then the article discusses some reasons young adults decided to remain committed to the local church. The report notes that 39 percent of those who stayed in the church said they felt involved in church activities, and 37 percent of those who stayed in the church said they felt committed to the mission.[1]

---

[1] Aaron Earls, "Most Teenagers Drop Out of Church When They Become Young Adults," Lifeway Research (website), January 15, 2019, https://research.lifeway.com/2019/01/15/most-teenagers-drop-out-of-church-as-young-adults/.

This goes to show that students are more likely to remain in the local church upon graduating from high school when they feel that they belong and have the relationships and opportunities to show for it.

The letter of 1 Peter reminds Christians of their identity in Christ and their responsibility to live for Christ in difficulty. Peter reminds them of the imminent return of Christ. So they must be ready. They must not give up.

Peter writes, "The end of all things is near" (1 Peter 4:7). Then he gives them a few areas to focus their attention on. In verse 7 he also tells them to pray. Then in verses 8 and 9 he tells them to love. They're sharing life! This is followed in verses 10 and 11 with a call to serve. And it's this focus on serving that we're going to consider in this chapter.

What does it mean to find your place?

To find your place means to discover your gift and to steward it well.

Peter says, "Just as each one has received a gift, use it to serve others, as good stewards of the varied grace of God" (v. 10).

By "gift," Peter is referring to a spiritual gift. And we read about spiritual gifts in other places of Scripture, including Romans 12:3–8, Ephesians 4:1–16, and 1 Corinthians 12:4–11.

If you're a believer, you have a gift. Peter says, "as each one has received a gift" (1 Peter 4:10). These gifts come from the same Spirit. In 1 Corinthians 12:4–6 Paul writes, "Now there are different gifts, but the same Spirit. There are different ministries, but the same Lord. And there are different activities, but the same God works all of them in each person."

So spiritual gifts come from God, and they are found in each believer.

You might be wondering, "What's my spiritual gift? How do I discover it?" Some believers have a good understanding of how God has gifted them. For others the idea of having a spiritual gift seems confusing.

I do believe there's a difference between spiritual gifts and what we call "talents" and "skills." Spiritual gifts are identified in God's Word.

In 1 Peter 4:10–11 Peter describes spiritual gifts as falling under the categories of speaking or serving. The spiritual gifts mentioned in Romans 12:3–8 include—

- Prophecy
- Service
- Teaching
- Exhortation
- Giving
- Leading
- Mercy

I'm not going to describe each of these in detail. But the Bible does show us what spiritual gifts are. Our talents and skills, on the other hand, include things like being athletic or artistic. So there's a distinction. But it's important to understand how God desires to use them all.

When it comes to discovering your spiritual gift, spiritual gift inventories that ask you questions and help you identify how God has gifted you are available. I've done

one before. I think they can be helpful to an extent. But the best way to discover your spiritual gift is to—well, serve in the life of the church!

You can serve in different areas of the church and learn to recognize how God has gifted you. The word Peter uses for *serve* can be translated as the verb *minister.* God has called you to minister. It's not just for pastors. As a believer and church member, you're gifted to minister in the church. Peter says we need to use those gifts as good stewards of God's varied grace. I love this. Peter is saying there are various gifts from the same God. And He has graced different believers in different ways to serve. It's important to use God's gifts in the way He intends. We must steward them well.

Spurgeon once said, "You are a steward. If a steward should receive his Lord's goods and keep them for himself, he would be an unfaithful steward. Child of God, see to it that you faithfully discharge your responsibility as one of the 'good stewards of the varied grace of God.'"[2]

We read about stewardship all throughout Scripture. In the previous chapter we considered good stewardship in the areas of our possessions and time. But 1 Peter 4:10–11 is a call to steward our spiritual gifts. And Peter gives us a couple of clear directives for how we can steward our gifts well in the local church.

To find your place means to steward your gift for the good of others.

Peter says, "Just as each one has received a gift, use it to serve others, as good stewards of the varied grace of

2 C. H. Spurgeon, *Spurgeon Commentary: 1 Peter*, ed. Elliot Ritzema (Bellingham, WA: Lexham Press, 2013), 1 Pet. 4:10.

God. If anyone speaks, let it be as one who speaks God's words; if anyone serves, let it be from the strength God provides" (vv. 10–11).

Our gifts aren't meant to be hoarded. Just as we must have open hands with our possessions and time for the advancement of God's mission, so we must have open hands with our gifts for the advancement of God's mission.

Our gifts encourage other believers. They edify other believers. And rather than turning inward and thinking about how we can make ourselves look good, we must be looking outward and asking, "How can I serve others?"

Thomas Schreiner writes, "Gifts are not given so that believers can congratulate themselves on their abilities. They are bestowed 'to serve others.'"[3]

It's an encouraging thought to consider how people in the church benefit from your gift. And as you discover your gift and begin stewarding it for the good of others, you begin realizing just how much you matter in the church.

For example, I discovered the gift of preaching as a teenager. God provided several opportunities for me to preach in several different churches. I quickly realized how using that gift in the church benefited my brothers and sisters in Christ. It was not because of me. It's not that I preached the best messages. It's that God worked through me to edify those churches and evangelize the lost.

Watching God use your gift in the church serves to encourage you. It reminds you of the valuable part you play in accomplishing His mission. It reminds you to

[3] Thomas R. Schreiner, *1 & 2 Peter and Jude*, Christian Standard Commentary (Nashville: Holman, 2020), 1 Pet. 4:10.

embrace your place and serve others with joy. Maybe it's not teaching or a type of leading. You might serve behind the scenes. But every single gift is needed in the church.

So we steward our gifts well when we use them for the good of others. But Peter also focuses our attention on the glory of God.

To find your place means to steward your gift for the glory of God.

Peter breaks into worship in verse 11: "If anyone speaks, let it be as one who speaks God's words; if anyone serves, let it be from the strength God provides, so that God may be glorified through Jesus Christ in everything. To him be the glory and the power forever and ever. Amen."

Our gifts are from God. They don't originate with us. And it's God who gets the glory when we steward them well. In 1 Corinthians 4:7 Paul asks, "What do you have that you didn't receive?"

There is truly something amazing about discovering how God has gifted you and helps you use that gift for the good of others. But it's even more amazing to recognize how using your gift glorifies Him. You're worshiping Him as you serve!

It's easy to lose sight of this as we're serving. It doesn't take much for us to have impure motives. Sometimes we serve from a place of insecurity. We try to find identity through our gifts rather than glorifying God through them.

You see, stewarding your gift for the glory of God is more than a project. It's not just community service. It's an opportunity for you to edify others in their walk with Christ. It's an opportunity to share Christ with those who don't know Him. And through it all, it's an opportunity to glorify the giver of every good and perfect gift.

Conclusion

Finding your place is key to accomplishing the mission of God. Unless believers are mobilized for ministry, they're unlikely to stick around for very long—much less live a missional life.

To find your place means to discover your gift and steward it well for the good of others and the glory of God. In my own experience I've seen that those who discover and steward their gifts in the local church are the ones who grow and go where God sends them. They understand the role their gifts play in God's mission. They're mobilized to live on mission. And that's the next part of the Multiply Model.

Questions

1. Have you discovered your spiritual gift(s)? If so, what did that discovery look like for you? If not, are you actively looking for it as you serve?
2. Has there ever been a time when you felt out of place? What was your response? Have you ever felt this way in the church?
3. Do you know what it's like to see others in the church benefit from your spiritual gift? Can you think of any examples in Scripture of God using the gift of someone to benefit another?
4. Why is it easy for us to lose sight of God's glory when we serve? What are some ways to keep it at the forefront of our minds as we operate in our gifts?

5. Have you ever been afraid to use your gift(s)? What does 2 Timothy 1:6–7 say?

Prayer Focus

Thank God for the opportunity you have to serve Him. Ask Him to help you recognize your gifts and steward them well.

6

Live on Mission

////////////////////////////////

Matthew 28:18–20

We're considering the last part of the Multiply Model, but it's wrong to say we're at the end of it. That defeats the purpose of multiplication.

The model has an arrow at the end for a reason. The goal isn't for discipleship to end with you. It's for you to be mobilized to make new disciples.

There comes a time when disciples of Jesus begin discipling others. They come to know God. They're shown what it means to share life. They're given opportunities to find their place. And before long, they're living on mission and making even more disciples!

This call to live on mission is clearly given to us in Matthew 28:18–20. In 2018 the Barna Group asked American churchgoers, "Have you heard of the Great Commission?" A total of 51 percent of them said they had never heard of it, while 25 percent said they had heard of it but couldn't remember what it means.[1]

You see, many Christians have become content with going to church and not making disciples. Some are willing to sit in a pew but not willing to sit at a table with someone and have a conversation about the gospel. The result of this mentality is maintenance, not multiplication.

If we're going to obey God and be disciples who make disciples, a willingness to go where God desires and evangelize those who don't know Him is required.

Let's study Matthew 28:18–20 and see what it means to live on mission.

To live on mission means to submit to Christ's authority.

Jesus tells His disciples to meet Him in Galilee (v. 10). When they come, He says something that should stop us dead in our tracks.

Verse 18 says, "Jesus came near and said to them, 'All authority has been given to me in heaven and on earth.'" Jesus is Lord. He is Master. He is King. That means we're not. And He has the right to tell us how to live our lives.

The authority of Jesus is clear in other places of the New Testament.

Matthew 7:28–29 says, "When Jesus had finished saying these things, the crowds were astonished at his teaching, because he was teaching them like one who had authority, and not like their scribes."

In John 17:1–2 we read, "Jesus spoke these things,

---

[1] "51% of Churchgoers Don't Know of the Great Commission," Barna Group (website), March 27, 2018, https://www.barna.com/research/half-churchgoers-not-heard-great-commission/.

looked up to heaven, and said, 'Father, the hour has come. Glorify your Son so that the Son may glorify you, since you gave him authority over all people, so that he may give eternal life to everyone you have given him.'"

After Jesus gives the Great Commission, He ascends to the right hand of the Father. He is highly exalted. Every knee will bow before Him. Every tongue will confess that He is Lord (Philippians 2:9–11).

If Jesus has all authority, that means we don't. He is the Master. And as we saw in chapter 2, we can't serve two masters. The Great Commission is so much more than Jesus giving us a good idea. It's more than simply a recommendation.

Most of us aren't prone to follow recommendations. Jordon got on to me the other day because I was driving faster than the yellow sign said I should. I responded, "It's just a recommendation! It's not the actual speed limit." Those advisory signs aren't enforced the same way. Most of us don't even notice them.

The words of Jesus in Matthew 28:18–20 aren't a suggestion. They're the real deal. Because He has all authority. Missional living is recognizing the authority Jesus has rather than clinging to what you think you can control.

Jesus says in Matthew 16:24–25, "If anyone wants to follow after me, let him deny himself, take up his cross, and follow me. For whoever wants to save his life will lose it, but whoever loses his life because of me will find it."

If we're going to live on mission, we must submit to the authority of Jesus rather than trying to keep our hands on the wheel of our lives. We must let go of our own plans to pursue God's plans.

To live on mission means to make disciples where Christ sends you.

The Great Commission continues: "Go, therefore, and make disciples of all nations, baptizing them in the name of the Father and of the Son and of the Holy Spirit, teaching them to observe everything I have commanded you" (vv. 19–20).

Jesus has a purpose for wherever He sends you. D. A. Carson says, "The aim of Jesus' disciples, therefore, is to make disciples of all men everywhere, without distinction."[2]

New disciples respond to the gospel in faith and repentance. They are saved by grace through faith in Christ. And we can expect them to eventually take the step of baptism as a symbol of their death to sin and new life in Jesus (Romans 6:4).

According to the Joshua Project, over 7,000 unreached people groups exist in the world today. An unreached people group is characterized by an inadequate number of indigenous Christians among the people who can evangelize them without outside help.[3]

The gospel is for all nations. The Great Commission is a great reminder for us of just how important it is to live on mission.

Not only are there unbelievers all around the world, but there are unbelievers around *us* every day. And we must make disciples where God sends us. For some, that looks like a place far away. For others, it looks like a hometown.

[2] D. A. Carson, *Matthew*, The Expositor's Bible Commentary, ed. Frank E. Gaebelein (Grand Rapids: Zondervan, 1984), 596.

[3] "Definitions: Unreached," Joshua Project (website), accessed October 21, 2023, https://joshuaproject.net/help/definitions#unreached.

Don't look down on where God sends you. But wherever He sends you, make disciples there. And when you live "sent," you live with an incomparable purpose.

I recently found an interesting article called "Don't Miss Gen Z's Missionary Potential," by Chip Bugnar. The Pew Research Center defines Gen Z as those born between 1997 and 2012.[4] That means I'm a Gen Z, and so are the students I pastor.

Bugnar mentions some of the common characteristics found in Gen Zers that make us great candidates for living on mission:

1. Gen Zers are attentive to ways the Lord may move them.
2. Gen Zers have relationships that transcend their physical locations.
3. Gen Zers feel the need to connect with people meaningfully.
4. Gen Zers are pressing into mental health.

To summarize his thoughts, Bugnar asks, "What if God has ordained certain Gen Z traits to be used for his redemptive purposes?"[5]

God is calling the teens and young adults of today to go and make disciples. He is calling us to live on mission. And this is truly the most satisfying life. It's easy to think we have better ideas than God does. But we don't. When

---

[4] Michael Dimock, "Defining Generations: Where Millennials End and Generation Z Begins," Pew Research Center (website), January 17, 2019, https://www.pewresearch.org/short-reads/2019/01/17/where-millennials-end-and-generation-z-begins/.

[5] Chip Bugnar, "Don't Miss Gen Z's Missionary Potential," The Gospel Coalition (website), September 3, 2023, https://www.thegospelcoalition.org/article/gen-zs-missionary-potential/.

we go where He sends us and live with a *multiply* mentality, we find true and lasting joy in Christ.

We're not promised an easy life. We might struggle. We might suffer. We may even die. But our hope in Jesus is secure. Nothing can take it away.

To live on mission means to remember Christ's presence.

At the end of the Great Commission Jesus says, "And remember, I am with you always, to the end of the age" (Matthew 28:20). Jesus is Immanuel, God with us (Matthew 1:23). And wherever He sends you, He is with you.

He doesn't send us somewhere to abandon us. He is with us. And His Spirit empowers us to live the life God calls us to live.

Maybe you realize that you're sent. But you're also scared. Throughout my life I've often found myself scared of where God was sending me. For example, I knew God was sending me to Cross Lanes Baptist Church in 2022 to be the student pastor. But I was scared. I knew I was young. I knew I didn't have a ton of experience. So I found myself sent and scared at the same time. But God is with us wherever He sends us—and that changes everything.

Jordon loves listening to Taylor Swift. One of the songs I often hear in the car is "You're on Your Own, Kid." It's not a Christian song by any means. But those words remind me of how thankful I am that Jesus doesn't leave me hanging.

It's not as if He sends you somewhere and says, "You're on your own, kid." Instead, His presence strengthens you to accomplish His mission.

We're often comforted when someone goes with us to

do something we feel inadequate to do. I can't tell you how many times I've asked my dad to come with me when taking my car to the shop. It's because I'm completely clueless. It's out of my comfort zone, and I'm easily taken advantage of in places like that.

If we find that much comfort from others in the littlest things of life, how much more should we be comforted by the very presence of Jesus who empowers us to accomplish God's mission?

Conclusion

The purpose of the arrow at the end of the Multiply Model is to communicate the idea of launching. It's to show the importance of going wherever God sends you. To live on mission means to submit to Christ's authority, to make disciples where He sends you, and to remember His presence.

The goal is for the model to be replicated as new disciples are made. But it's also important to keep in mind that while the Multiply Model leads to living on mission, you and I never get past the other three parts.

You never get past knowing God. You must continually seek Him. It's all for His glory. He is making you more and more like Jesus as you abide in Him. In fact, it's only by abiding in Jesus that your life can produce gospel fruit (John 15:4–5). You never get past sharing your life. Gospel community is essential for new Christians and mature Christians alike. You never get past finding your place in the life of the church. Stewarding your gifts for ministry mobilizes you to live on mission.

So we've considered the mission. We've worked through a gospel-shaped model for accomplishing it. Now, in the final part of the book, let's think some more about the move God is calling you to make.

Questions

1. Has there ever been a time when you knew God was sending you somewhere but it scared you? Did you stay or go?
2. What is your experience with evangelism? Why is it important?
3. Have you ever viewed God's mission as a recommendation? What characterizes our lives when we view it that way?
4. Have you experienced the joy of discipling someone else? Can you think of someone in your life whom God is calling you to disciple?
5. How does the presence of Jesus and the power of the Spirit make a difference in your daily life?

Prayer Focus

Thank God for using you in accomplishing His mission. Ask Him to give you opportunities to share the gospel with others and to disciple them.

The Move

7

Live Out Your Calling

//////////////////////////////

1 Corinthians 7:17–24

The next chapter is a call to action. So is this current chapter. But it's primarily meant to clarify some misconceptions you might have about what it means to live on mission.

You don't need to change your status to live out your calling. First Corinthians 7:17 is one of my favorite verses in the Bible. Paul writes, "Let each one live his life in the situation the Lord assigned when God called him. This is what I command in all the churches."

The verse occurs in the context of marriage and singleness. Paul himself was single. And he encouraged singleness in 1 Corinthians 7:7. Apparently some Corinthians had misunderstood and thought being single produced a higher degree of spirituality in their lives. So some sought a change in status.

But a married person can live on mission just as a single person can. A teacher can live on mission just as a missionary can. A plumber can live on mission just as a pastor can.

Of course, God may call you to marry someone if you're currently single. He may call you to serve Him as a pastor or missionary. But none of that changes the fact that you're called to live on mission in whatever status you currently have.

Let me show you a few reasons why.

Your identity is in Christ, not in your status.

Paul had already said in 1 Corinthians 1:9, "God is faithful; you were called by him into fellowship with his Son, Jesus Christ our Lord."

Some of them were single when called to Christ. Some were married. Some were widowed. Some were engaged. But it didn't make a difference because the status didn't define the identity of the person who believed. Rather, Christ did.

In 1 Corinthians 7:24 Paul restates his point when he says, "Brothers and sisters, each person is to remain with God in the situation in which he was called." Sandwiched between verse 17 and verse 24 are a couple of examples Paul uses to strengthen his point. The first illustration is circumcision. The second is Greco-Roman servanthood.

Paul's illustrations refer to background and occupation. You may be able to change your status—but that's not necessary in order to be successful in your calling as a child of God.

In his commentary Gordon Fee writes, "Change may occur, but one's calling in Christ means that change is unnecessary, and certainly not to be a compulsion."[1]

We often identify ourselves by a status. Think about the statements we make that begin with "I am a . . ." For example, "I am a husband." "I am a dad." "I am a pastor."

You might give some of the following responses:

- "I am a student."
- "I am a soccer player."
- "I am an accountant."

It's not that those things are wrong. But your identity runs deeper than that. As a believer, you find your identity in Christ—regardless of your status. I love what Paul writes in Ephesians 2:10: "We are his workmanship, created in Christ Jesus for good works, which God prepared ahead of time for us to do."

We work *from* identity, not *for* identity. Your identity is in Christ, not in your status.

Your pursuit is Christ, not your status.

Let's think about the illustrations Paul uses to strengthen his point. Circumcision was a defining mark for God's people. The Jews were circumcised. Gentiles were also expected to endure circumcision to belong. But Paul debunked that argument.

He writes, "Was anyone already circumcised when he

---

[1] Gordon Fee, *The First Epistle to the Corinthians*, The New International Commentary on the New Testament, Revised ed. (Grand Rapids: Eerdmans, 2014), 352.

was called? He should not undo his circumcision. Was anyone called while uncircumcised? He should not get circumcised. Circumcision does not matter and uncircumcision does not matter. Keeping God's commands is what matters. Let each of you remain in the situation in which he was called" (vv. 18–20).

There was no need to be circumcised because it made no difference in their identity as children of God. In Galatians 5:6 Paul writes, "In Christ Jesus neither circumcision nor uncircumcision accomplishes anything; what matters is faith working through love."

Then Paul highlights servanthood. He is referring here to a humble type of occupation. Even though it was the lowest social status a person could have, it provided a way for people to have a steady job, a means to meet their needs.

Paul encouraged a servant to change his or her status if possible. But it didn't make a difference in the person's identity as a child of God.

In fact, Jesus emphasized the importance of servanthood in Matthew 20:25–26 when He told His disciples, "You know that the rulers of the Gentiles lord it over them, and those in high positions act as tyrants over them. It must not be like that among you. On the contrary, whoever wants to become great among you must be your servant."

We are servants of Christ—regardless of our earthly status. We belong to Him. And we should pursue Him above any change in status.

So how does this apply to us today? There's nothing wrong with pursuing a particular occupation. It's okay if you want to be married one day. It's okay if you want to remain single. And choosing one thing over another doesn't make you a second-class Christian.

But your pursuit must be Christ above any change in status. Remember—you're being conformed to His image.

Your status is irrelevant to Godly success.

The Corinthians didn't need to change their marital statuses to be successful as believers. They didn't need to be circumcised to be successful. Nor did they need to change their occupations. In whatever situation they were called, Paul encouraged them to remain with God and pursue Christ.

Status is irrelevant to success. I want to spend a moment explaining this because it's not what culture teaches.

First, it's important for us to define what biblical success is. Let me tell you about a parable Jesus shared in Matthew 25. It's called "the parable of the talents." Jesus said a man went on a journey and entrusted his possessions to three servants. But he gave each of the servants a different number of resources. He gave the first servant five talents, the second servant two talents, and the third servant one talent. Then the man departed.

The guy with five talents worked to double his amount, leaving him with ten. The guy with two talents also worked to double his amount, leaving him with four. But the guy with one talent dug a hole in the ground and hid it because he was afraid of losing it.

When the master returned, he told the guy with ten talents, "Well done, good and faithful servant!" In the same way he told the guy with four talents, "Well done, good and faithful servant!" But when the guy with one talent approached the master, the master said, "You evil, lazy servant!"

We learn a lot about God's understanding of success from this parable. Success is being faithful with whatever God entrusts to you. Jesus called the last guy lazy. It was not because he had the least but because he wasn't faithful with what he had. And the first guy was called successful. It was not because he had the most but because he was faithful with what he had.

This is not the way we often think. We see someone dressed in dirty clothes and working a dirty job and think, "Oh, he must be lazy." We see someone dressed in a suit and working in a skyscraper and think, "Oh, he must be successful." But that's not what we find in God's Word. The person working the dirty job might be more successful than the rich businessman. Because it's not about how much or how little—it's about how faithful.

Paul wanted the Corinthian believers to realize how status is irrelevant to success as a child of God.

You can be faithful with little or much, as a minimum-wage worker or as a supervisor, as a husband or as a single guy, as a single girl or as a wife. Godly success is about being faithful with what God gives you—not your status.

In his book *God at Work* Gene Edward Veith Jr. writes, "It is important to remember in understanding vocation that He [God] does not operate as the world does, that He may call us to what the world and what we ourselves might consider a position that is 'beneath us,' lacking the glamour and importance that we would like for ourselves."[2]

---

[2] Gene Edward Veith Jr., *God at Work: Your Christian Vocation in All of Life*, Redesign ed. (Wheaton, IL: Crossway, 2002), 70–71.

You don't need to be a pastor to be successful as a child of God. You don't need to be a long-term missionary to be successful as a child of God. You don't need to be a doctor, lawyer, or CEO to be successful as a child of God. You can be a garbage truck driver. You can work at a gas station. You can be a plumber and be successful as a child of God. Because it's not about the status—it's about faithfulness.

Conclusion

A life on mission for the gospel is a life for you. It doesn't require you to fit a certain mold. It requires only that you know and follow Jesus Christ by grace through faith.

Maybe He is calling you to be a pastor or missionary. Maybe He is calling you to marry or remain single. But you can live out your calling successfully in whatever status you find yourself until God leads you to change it—if He ever does.

So live out your calling! The next chapter is meant to help you take that step.

Questions

1. Maybe you've thought, *I'll live on mission when _____* (fill in the blank). Can you think of some reasons you're tempted to put it off?
2. How does your identity in Christ influence the statuses you have in this life? What happens when you value a status more than Christ?
3. Read Matthew 20:28 and Philippians 2:5–8. How does the example of Jesus impact your understanding of status and success?
4. Do you believe God is calling you to a different status?

For example, maybe you feel called to ministry. Be sure to talk to someone about it!

5. How can you live out your calling in the statuses you currently have?

Prayer Focus

Thank God for the secure identity you have in Jesus Christ. Ask Him to help you live out your calling in the assignment you have today and in whatever assignments He may give you later.

8

Take a Step

Acts 1:9–14

We're returning to Acts 1. The disciples receive the mission in verse 8. Then in verses 9–14 the disciples make a move.

The mission is given on the Mount of Olives, where Jesus ascends to the Father. Talk about a mountaintop experience!

My family recently hiked to Dream Lake in Rocky Mountain National Park, in northern Colorado. Dayton enjoyed the ride in his child carrier on my back. Our younger boy, Shepherd, enjoyed the ride in Jordon's womb. But it was a difficult hike for me and especially Jordon, who was six months pregnant!

When we finally made it to the top, the view was truly breathtaking. It was early May, and the lake was still frozen and snow still covered the ground. We just stood there for a while admiring the beauty. We took as many pictures as we could while Dayton ate a Clif Bar.

In moments like that, we're speechless. Lost in the moment. Even a bit overwhelmed. On the mountain everything looks so clear. We're encouraged and invigorated—until we remember that we can't stay there forever.

No matter how long we try to make it last, we eventually need to climb back down the mountain. And we know the way. So we take a step and begin the descent. Before long we're back to the ordinary.

You see, the mountaintop experience of the disciples in Acts 1 is a lot like this. Only, they see something even more beautiful and breathtaking—the ascension of Jesus Christ.

Acts 1:10 says the disciples gazed into heaven as Jesus ascended—until two men in white clothes stood beside them and gave them a wake-up call. In verse 11 they said, "Men of Galilee, why do you stand looking up into heaven? This same Jesus, who has been taken from you into heaven, will come in the same way that you have seen him going into heaven." They can't gaze into the sky forever. And they know it because they have a mission. They have a clear step to take. As you come to the end of this book, maybe you're asking the question "Now what?" You've read a lot about the mission of God. You've considered what it means to know God, share your life, find your place, and live on mission. But you haven't taken a step.

I want to help you take the next step God is calling you to take as you wrestle with the mission of God. So what does it look like to take a step?

Take a step of faith in
response to God's mission.

Hebrews 11:1 says, "Now faith is the reality of what is hoped for, the proof of what is not seen." Then, in verse 6, the author of Hebrews writes, "Now without faith it is impossible to please God, since the one who draws near to him must believe that he exists and that he rewards those who seek him."

It takes faith to respond as God desires. The disciples are aware of God's plan. They're given a promise. They know the Holy Spirit is coming. And they respond by taking a step of faith.

John Stott says, "You have seen Jesus go. You will see him come. But between that going and coming there must be another. The Spirit must come, and you must go—into the world for Christ."[1]

I don't know the step God is calling you to take. But it's going to take faith. And you might be tempted to stay where you are. Maybe you're hesitating. Trying to hold on to what you think you can control when you know God is calling you to let go.

You've considered God's mission and how it's accomplished. And there's a step you know you need to take.

Perhaps you don't know God. You don't have a relationship with Him. If that's you, the step you must take is one of faith and repentance. It's one of turning from sin and turning toward God. It's trusting in the finished work of Christ upon the cross on your behalf. This is where it starts.

Maybe you do know God as did the early disciples in

---

[1] John Stott, *The Message of Acts*, The Bible Speaks Today, ed. John Stott (Downers Grove, IL: InterVarsity Press, 1990), 23.

Acts 1. You've come to Him in faith. And you're grateful for His mission. You're grateful He seeks to save the lost. Yet as you consider His mission, you realize He wants to use you in accomplishing it. For a long time you've viewed yourself as only a disciple. But you realize that as a disciple you're supposed to make more disciples. You're called to multiplication.

Maybe God is calling you to respond by sharing your life with other believers more than you currently are. Maybe God is calling you to respond by becoming a better steward of His gifts by finding your place.

The step to engage in gospel community takes faith. The step to become a better steward takes faith. But the mission of God is worth taking that step. It's a mission worth giving your life to.

Take a step of faith in the direction God sends.

The disciples knew where to go. Acts 1:12–14 explains, "Then they returned to Jerusalem from the Mount of Olives, which is near Jerusalem—a Sabbath day's journey away. When they arrived, they went to the room upstairs where they were staying: Peter, John, James, Andrew, Philip, Thomas, Bartholomew, Matthew, James the son of Alphaeus, Simon the Zealot, and Judas the son of James."

Remember—Jesus told His followers in verse 8 to begin making disciples in Jerusalem. He told them in verse 4 to stay in Jerusalem until the promised Holy Spirit empowered them. So they took a step of faith in the direction of Jerusalem. When they arrived they gathered in an upper room. And Luke gives us an attendance sheet of the disciples who were present.

There are eleven of them. Of course, Judas Iscariot was no longer there. As we're going to see in a moment, they were about to choose a replacement for Judas. But let's consider what it means for us to step according to God's direction as we respond to His mission.

Just because you know the direction doesn't mean you know the details. This is so important for you to realize, especially as it pertains to understanding God's will and the steps He calls you to take. The early disciples of Jesus knew the direction to go. But they did not know every detail of what life will be like in Jerusalem and what they would experience there.

One of the reasons we often hesitate or even neglect to take a step of faith in the direction God desires is that we feel as if we need to know the details.

For example, let's say God is sending you to live on mission at a particular university. It's clear to you. You know God wants you to join Him on mission there. And He is calling you to take a step of faith in that direction.

But you don't know what God wants you to major in. You don't know what your housing situation will be like. You don't know what types of temptations or persecutions you might face. So rather than taking a step in that direction, you try to suppress it or even neglect it.

But you may not need to know those details quite yet. They come in due time. There is, however, a clarity of direction. As you follow God's plan, He shows you what else you need to know when you need to know it. In their excellent book *Calling Out the Called*, Scott Pace and Shane Pruitt write, "We want to know what the future holds, including where we will serve, what our specific ministry responsibilities will include, and how the Lord will use us. While we should be hopeful, these unknown details are not necessary to determine our next steps."[2]

Abraham had a vague idea of where God was leading him. He journeyed into Canaan with no details and hardly any direction. But he obeyed. He took a step of faith. And God provided what He needed when He needed it.

The author of Hebrews describes the faith of Abraham when he writes in 11:8, "By faith Abraham, when he was called, obeyed and set out for a place that he was going to receive as an inheritance. He went out, even though he did not know where he was going."

We must take a step of faith in the direction God sends.

Take a step of faith with prayerful dependence.

The early followers of Jesus went to Jerusalem and gathered in an upper room. Then, verse 14 says, "They were continually united in prayer, along with the women, including Mary the mother of Jesus, and his brothers."

The context of Acts 1 and 2 is super-important here. Their persistent prayer is especially important for at least two reasons.

First, they know the Holy Spirit is about to come. Jesus told them not to leave Jerusalem until the Spirit came. And He came in Acts 2. Second, as verses 15–26 explain, they were about to choose a twelfth disciple to replace Judas.

So there was clearly a need for them to pray with a dependence on God. They needed power to carry out the

---

[2] Scott Pace and Shane Pruitt, *Calling Out the Called: Discipling Those Called to Ministry Leadership* (Nashville: B&H Publishing Group, 2022), 25.

mission of God—because they couldn't do it on their own. And neither can we.

Those of us who know God have the Spirit of God. And we must rely on Him to be the disciple-makers He calls us to be. The same can be said of those early followers of Christ.

They needed wisdom. And this is especially found in their desperate prayer for who should replace Judas as an apostle. The prayer is found in verses 24 and 25: "Then they prayed, 'You, Lord, know everyone's hearts; show which of these two you have chosen to take the place in this apostolic ministry that Judas left to go where he belongs.'"

Matthias was chosen.

As you take a step of faith in response to God's mission, don't forget your desperate need for the power and wisdom God provides. God's mission is greater than your own strength and wisdom.

I'm reminded of what James writes in James 1:5: "Now if any of you lacks wisdom, he should ask God—who gives to all generously and ungrudgingly—and it will be given to him."

So take heart, because no matter what step God is calling you to take, His power and wisdom are available to you. These are not things you can somehow find within yourself. But you can count on Him and be dependent on Him. You can prayerfully seek Him and the strength He provides.

I love the following quote by A. C. Dixon: "When we depend upon organizations, we get what organizations can do; when we depend upon education, we get what education can do; when we depend upon man, we get what man can do; but when we depend upon prayer, we get what God can do."[3]

It's time to take a step. But don't take a prayerless one.

Conclusion

God has a mission. And He invites you to join Him on that mission. In response to God's mission, take a step of faith in the direction He sends with prayerful dependence.

By now that step is probably clear to you. Is there a gift you're not using? Is there gospel community you're avoiding? Are you unwilling to commit to a local church? Are you trying to avoid baptism? Is there someone you need to share Christ with? Maybe you simply need to know God for yourself!

God is working. He is accomplishing His mission in the world. He is the multiplier. It's He who gives the growth (1 Corinthians 3:6). It's He who produces much fruit and gets the glory as we abide in Christ (John 15:8).

Wherever you are in the journey, I pray you take the next step. May He use you to make disciples who make disciples. May He use you to grow His forever family—until the day when a multitude from every nation, tribe, people, and language stand before His throne (Revelation 7:9–10).

It's time to *multiply*!

Questions

1. As you think about the message of this book, what stands out to you the most?
2. What direction is God calling you to go? What details

---

[3] Quoted in John Piper, *Brothers, We Are Not Professionals: A Plea to Pastors for Radical Ministry*, Revised ed. (Nashville: B&H Publishing Group, 2013), 68.

are you uncertain about?

3. Compare 2 Corinthians 5:7 with Hebrews 11:1, 6. What does it look like for you to walk by faith?

4. Read 1 Thessalonians 5:17. What does it look like for you to walk in prayerful dependence?

5. God is the one who saves. He is the one who multiplies. His plan will be accomplished. How does this give you confidence in taking the step you know you need to take?

Prayer Focus

Thank God for the certainty of His mission being accomplished. Ask Him to strengthen your faith and deepen your prayers as you step in the direction He sends you.

Sycamore
S T O R I E S

Helping People See Jesus
sycamorestories.org

www.ingramcontent.com/pod-product-compliance
Lightning Source LLC
La Vergne TN
LVHW041202080426
835511LV00006B/706